MY SERMON NOTES

A Prayer Journal & Church Activity Book for Kids

MY SERMON NOTES

Name:_____

date:_____

speaker:_____

passages:_____

TODAY'S SERMON IS ABOUT:

Say WHAT?!
Two★ things i DIDN'T understand:

?

?

WORSHIP WORDS
(COLOR EACH OF THE WORDS YOU HEARD TODAY)

JESUS	LOVE
PRAY	FAITH
BIBLE	GOD
OBEY	TRUTH
PEACE	CROSS
FORGIVE	SIN
HOLY	CHURCH
HEAVEN	LORD

CHURCH DOODLES

Something That Inspired Me From Today's Sermon

SONGS WE SANG TODAY

I'm SO Thankful For:

PRAYER requests

_____
_____
_____
_____
_____
_____

How I Felt About Today's Service

SERMON NOTES

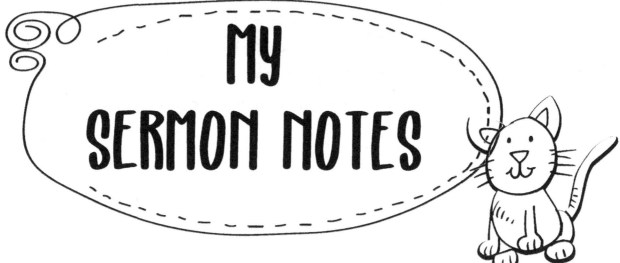

MY SERMON NOTES

Name:_____ Speaker:_____

date:_____ passages:_____

TODAY'S SERMON IS ABOUT:

SAY WHAT?!
Two⊛ things i DiDn't unDeRstanD:

? _____
_____
_____
? _____
_____

WORSHIP WORDS
(COLOR EACH OF THE WORDS YOU HEARD TODAY)

JESUS   LOVE
PRAY   FAITH
BIBLE   GOD
OBEY   TRUTH
PEACE   CROSS
FORGIVE   SIN
HOLY   CHURCH
HEAVEN   LORD

CHURCH DOODLES

Something That Inspired Me From Today's Sermon

♪♫ SONGS WE SANG TODAY

I'm SO Thankful For:

PRAYER requests

_____
_____
_____
_____
_____
_____

How I Felt About Today's Service

SERMON NOTES

MY SERMON NOTES

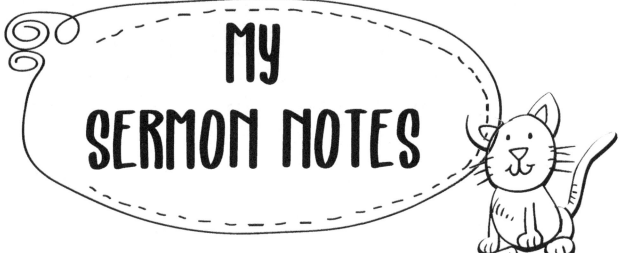

Name:_____

date:_____

Speaker:_____

Passages:_____

TODAY'S SERMON IS ABOUT:

_____

_____

_____

_____

SAY WHAT?!
TWO⊛ things i DIDN'T UNDERSTAND:

? _____

_____

? _____

_____

WORSHIP WORDS
(COLOR EACH OF THE WORDS YOU HEARD TODAY)

JESUS   LOVE

PRAY   FAITH

BIBLE   GOD

OBEY   TRUTH

PEACE   CROSS

FORGIVE   SIN

HOLY   CHURCH

HEAVEN   LORD

CHURCH DOODLES

Something That Inspired Me From Today's Sermon

SONGS WE SANG TODAY

I'm SO Thankful For:

PRAYER requests

_____
_____
_____
_____
_____
_____

How I Felt About Today's Service

SERMON NOTES

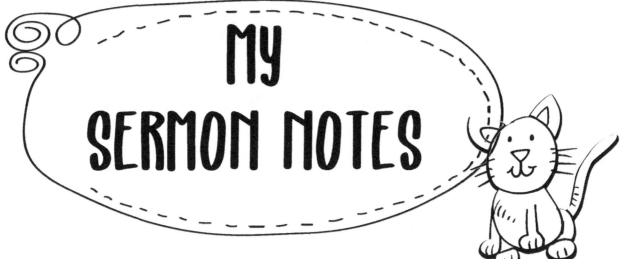

MY SERMON NOTES

Name:_____   Speaker:_____

date:_____   passages:_____

TODAY'S SERMON IS ABOUT:

Say WHAT?!
Two✴ things i DiDn't unDerstanD:

? _____

_____

? _____

_____

WORSHIP WORDS
(COLOR EACH OF THE WORDS YOU HEARD TODAY)

JESUS   LOVE

PRAY   FAITH

BIBLE   GOD

OBEY   TRUTH

PEACE   CROSS

FORGIVE SIN

HOLY   CHURCH

HEAVEN LORD

CHURCH DOODLES

Something That Inspired Me From Today's Sermon

SONGS WE SANG TODAY

I'm SO Thankful For:

PRAYER REQUESTS

_____
_____
_____
_____
_____

How I Felt About Today's Service

SERMON NOTES

_____

_____

_____

_____

_____

_____

_____

_____

_____

_____

_____

_____

_____

_____

_____

_____

_____

_____

_____

_____

_____

_____

_____

_____

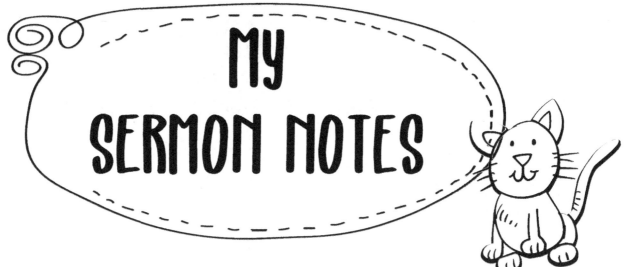

MY SERMON NOTES

Name: _____

date: _____

speaker: _____

passages: _____

TODAY'S SERMON IS ABOUT:

Say WHAT?!
Two✱ things i DiDN't uNDeRstaND:

? _____

? _____

WORSHIP WORDS
(COLOR EACH OF THE WORDS YOU HEARD TODAY)

JESUS   LOVE

PRAY   FAITH

BIBLE   GOD

OBEY   TRUTH

PEACE   CROSS

FORGIVE   SIN

HOLY   CHURCH

HEAVEN   LORD

CHURCH DOODLES

Something That Inspired Me From Today's Sermon

SONGS WE SANG TODAY

I'm SO Thankful For:

PRAYER requests

How I Felt About Today's Service

SERMON NOTES

_____
_____
_____
_____
_____
_____
_____
_____
_____
_____
_____
_____
_____
_____
_____
_____
_____
_____
_____
_____
_____
_____
_____
_____
_____
_____
_____
_____

MY SERMON NOTES

Name: _____

date: _____

Speaker: _____

passages: _____

TODAY'S SERMON IS ABOUT:

_____

_____

_____

_____

SAY WHAT?!
Two✪ things i didn't understand:

? _____

_____

? _____

_____

WORSHIP WORDS
(COLOR EACH OF THE WORDS YOU HEARD TODAY)

JESUS   LOVE

PRAY   FAITH

BIBLE   GOD

OBEY   TRUTH

PEACE   CROSS

FORGIVE   SIN

HOLY   CHURCH

HEAVEN   LORD

CHURCH DOODLES

Something That Inspired Me From Today's Sermon

SONGS WE SANG TODAY

I'm SO Thankful For:

PRAYER requests

_____
_____
_____
_____
_____

How I Felt About Today's Service

SERMON NOTES

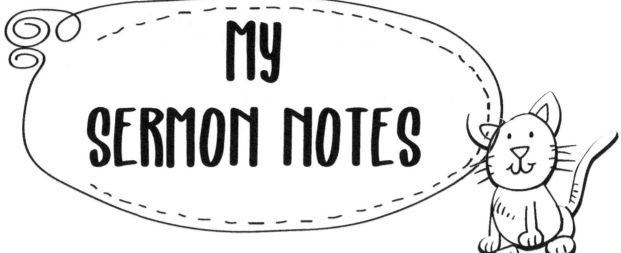

MY SERMON NOTES

Name:_____

date:_____

speaker:_____

passages:_____

TODAY'S SERMON IS ABOUT:

SAY WHAT?!
TWO⊛ things i Didn't understand:

? _____

? _____

WORSHIP WORDS
(COLOR EACH OF THE WORDS YOU HEARD TODAY)

JESUS   LOVE
PRAY   FAITH
BIBLE   GOD
OBEY   TRUTH
PEACE   CROSS
FORGIVE   SIN
HOLY   CHURCH
HEAVEN   LORD

CHURCH DOODLES

Something That Inspired Me From Today's Sermon

SONGS WE SANG TODAY

I'm SO Thankful For:

PRAYER requests

_____
_____
_____
_____
_____
_____

How I Felt About Today's Service

SERMON NOTES

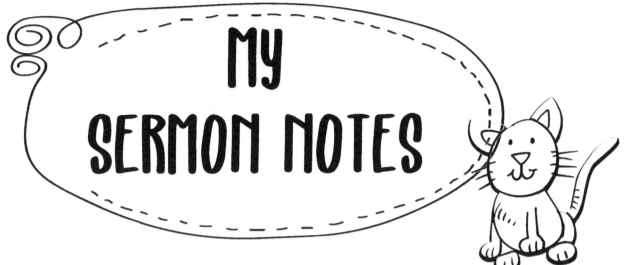

MY SERMON NOTES

Name:_____   Speaker:_____
date:_____   passages:_____

TODAY'S SERMON IS ABOUT:
_____
_____
_____
_____

SAY WHAT?!
Tw⊛ things i DiDn't unDeRstanD:

? _____

? _____

WORSHIP WORDS
(COLOR EACH OF THE WORDS YOU HEARD TODAY)

JESUS   LOVE
PRAY   FAITH
BIBLE   GOD
OBEY   TRUTH
PEACE   CROSS
FORGIVE   SIN
HOLY   CHURCH
HEAVEN   LORD

CHURCH DOODLES

Something That Inspired Me From Today's Sermon

SONGS WE SANG TODAY

I'm SO Thankful For:

PRAYER requests

_____
_____
_____
_____
_____
_____

How I Felt About Today's Service

SERMON NOTES

MY SERMON NOTES

Name:_____

date:_____

speaker:_____

passages:_____

TODAY'S SERMON IS ABOUT:

SAY WHAT?!
TWO★ things i DIDN'T UNDERSTAND:

?

?

WORSHIP WORDS
(COLOR EACH OF THE WORDS YOU HEARD TODAY)

JESUS   LOVE

PRAY   FAITH

BIBLE   GOD

OBEY   TRUTH

PEACE   CROSS

FORGIVE   SIN

HOLY   CHURCH

HEAVEN   LORD

CHURCH DOODLES

Something That Inspired Me From Today's Sermon

SONGS WE SANG TODAY

I'm SO Thankful For:

PRAYER requests

_____

_____

_____

_____

_____

_____

How I Felt About Today's Service

SERMON NOTES

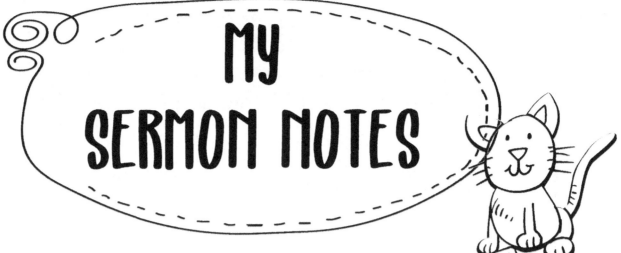

MY SERMON NOTES

Name:_____

date:_____

speaker:_____

passages:_____

TODAY'S SERMON IS ABOUT:

_____

_____

_____

_____

SAY WHAT?!
Tw⊛ things i DiDn't unDerstanD:

?_____

_____

?_____

_____

WORSHIP WORDS
(COLOR EACH OF THE WORDS YOU HEARD TODAY)

JESUS	LOVE
PRAY	FAITH
BIBLE	GOD
OBEY	TRUTH
PEACE	CROSS
FORGIVE	SIN
HOLY	CHURCH
HEAVEN	LORD

CHURCH DOODLES

Something That Inspired Me From Today's Sermon

SONGS WE SANG TODAY

I'm SO Thankful For:

PRAYER requests

_____
_____
_____
_____
_____
_____

How I Felt About Today's Service

SERMON NOTES

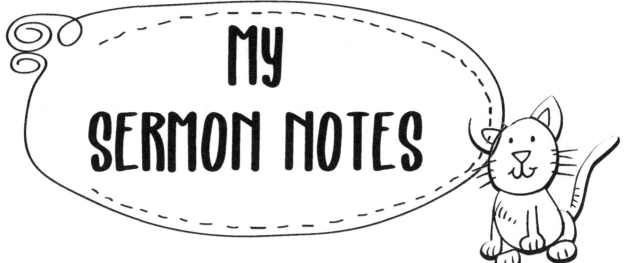

MY SERMON NOTES

Name:_____   Speaker:_____
date:_____   passages:_____

TODAY'S SERMON IS ABOUT:

SAY WHAT?!
Two★ things i DiDn't understand:

? _____
  _____
? _____
  _____

WORSHIP WORDS
(COLOR EACH OF THE WORDS YOU HEARD TODAY)

JESUS   LOVE
PRAY   FAITH
BIBLE   GOD
OBEY   TRUTH
PEACE   CROSS
FORGIVE   SIN
HOLY   CHURCH
HEAVEN   LORD

CHURCH DOODLES

Something That Inspired Me From Today's Sermon

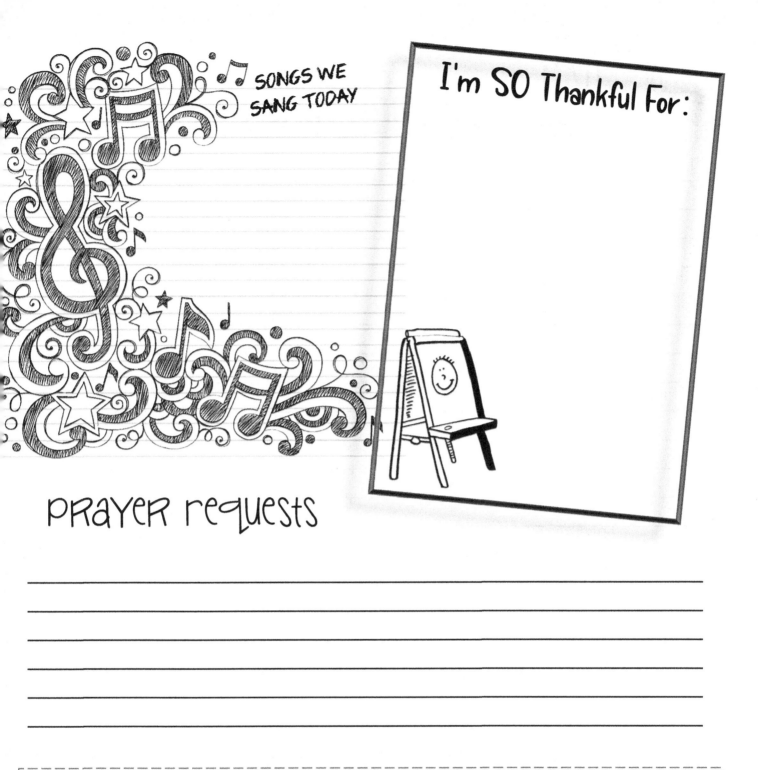

SONGS WE SANG TODAY

I'm SO Thankful For:

PRAYER requests

_____
_____
_____
_____
_____
_____

How I Felt About Today's Service

SERMON NOTES

_____
_____
_____
_____
_____
_____
_____
_____
_____
_____
_____
_____
_____
_____
_____
_____
_____
_____
_____
_____
_____
_____
_____
_____
_____
_____
_____

MY SERMON NOTES

Name:_____

date:_____

Speaker:_____

passages:_____

TODAY'S SERMON IS ABOUT:

_____

_____

_____

_____

SAY WHAT?!
Two✷ things i didn't understand:

? _____

_____

_____

? _____

_____

WORSHIP WORDS
(COLOR EACH OF THE WORDS YOU HEARD TODAY)

JESUS   LOVE
PRAY   FAITH
BIBLE   GOD
OBEY   TRUTH
PEACE   CROSS
FORGIVE   SIN
HOLY   CHURCH
HEAVEN   LORD

CHURCH DOODLES

Something That Inspired Me From Today's Sermon

SONGS WE
SANG TODAY

I'm SO Thankful For:

PRAYER requests

_____
_____
_____
_____
_____
_____

How I Felt About Today's Service

SERMON NOTES

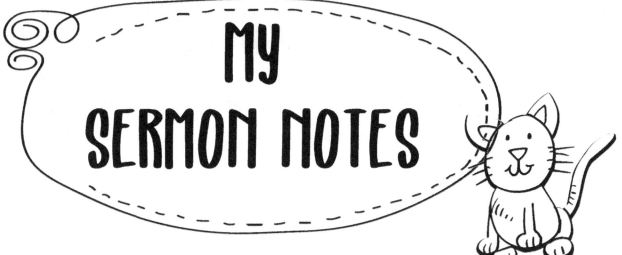

MY SERMON NOTES

Name: _____

date: _____

Speaker: _____

passages: _____

TODAY'S SERMON IS ABOUT:

_____

_____

_____

_____

Say WHAT?!
Two⊛ things i Didn't understand:

? _____

_____

? _____

_____

WORSHIP WORDS
(COLOR EACH OF THE WORDS YOU HEARD TODAY)

JESUS	LOVE
PRAY	FAITH
BIBLE	GOD
OBEY	TRUTH
PEACE	CROSS
FORGIVE	SIN
HOLY	CHURCH
HEAVEN	LORD

CHURCH DOODLES

Something That Inspired Me From Today's Sermon

SONGS WE SANG TODAY

I'm SO Thankful For:

PRAYER REQUESTS

_____
_____
_____
_____
_____
_____

How I Felt About Today's Service

SERMON NOTES

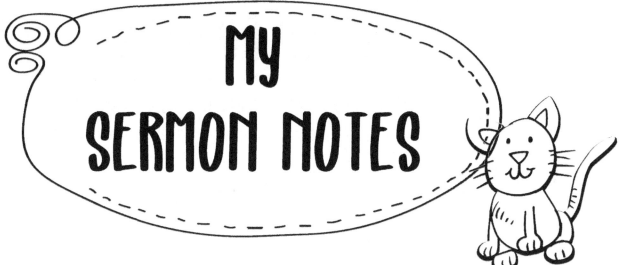

MY SERMON NOTES

Name:_____   Speaker:_____
date:_____   passages:_____

TODAY'S SERMON IS ABOUT:

_____
_____
_____
_____

Say WHAT?!
TW❋ things i DiDn't UnDerstanD:

? _____
  _____
  _____
? _____
  _____

WORSHIP WORDS
(COLOR EACH OF THE WORDS YOU HEARD TODAY)

JESUS   LOVE
PRAY   FAITH
BIBLE   GOD
OBEY   TRUTH
PEACE   CROSS
FORGIVE   SIN
HOLY   CHURCH
HEAVEN   LORD

CHURCH DOODLES

Something That Inspired Me From Today's Sermon

SONGS WE SANG TODAY

I'm SO Thankful For:

PRAYER requests

_____
_____
_____
_____
_____

How I Felt About Today's Service

SERMON NOTES

MY SERMON NOTES

Name:_____ Speaker:_____

date:_____ passages:_____

TODAY'S SERMON IS ABOUT:

_____

_____

_____

_____

Say WHAT?!
Tw⊛ things i DIDN'T understand:

? _____

_____

? _____

_____

WORSHIP WORDS
(COLOR EACH OF THE WORDS YOU HEARD TODAY)

JESUS   LOVE

PRAY   FAITH

BIBLE   GOD

OBEY   TRUTH

PEACE   CROSS

FORGIVE   SIN

HOLY   CHURCH

HEAVEN   LORD

CHURCH DOODLES

Something That Inspired Me From Today's Sermon

SONGS WE SANG TODAY

I'm SO Thankful For:

PRAYER requests

_____
_____
_____
_____
_____
_____

How I Felt About Today's Service

SERMON NOTES

MY SERMON NOTES

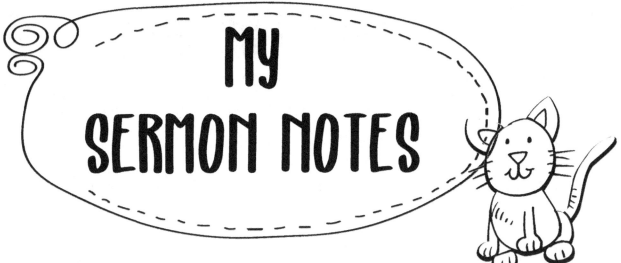

Name:_____   Speaker:_____
date:_____   passages:_____

TODAY'S SERMON IS ABOUT:

SAY WHAT?!
Two⊛ things i Didn't understand:

? _____
  _____
? _____
  _____

WORSHIP WORDS
(COLOR EACH OF THE WORDS YOU HEARD TODAY)

JESUS   LOVE
PRAY   FAITH
BIBLE   GOD
OBEY   TRUTH
PEACE   CROSS
FORGIVE   SIN
HOLY   CHURCH
HEAVEN   LORD

CHURCH DOODLES

Something That Inspired Me From Today's Sermon

SONGS WE SANG TODAY

I'm SO Thankful For:

PRAYER requests

_____
_____
_____
_____
_____
_____

How I Felt About Today's Service

SERMON NOTES

MY SERMON NOTES

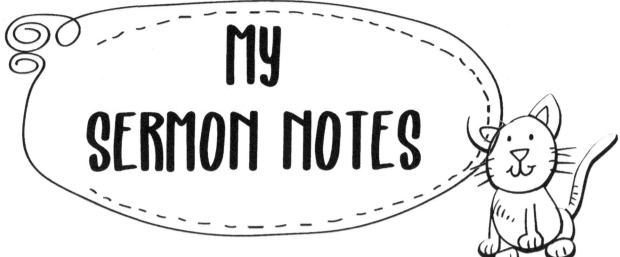

Name:_____

date:_____

Speaker:_____

passages:_____

TODAY'S SERMON IS ABOUT:

Say WHAT?!
Two✷ things i DiDn't UNDerSTanD:

? _____

? _____

WORSHIP WORDS
(COLOR EACH OF THE WORDS YOU HEARD TODAY)

JESUS   LOVE

PRAY   FAITH

BIBLE   GOD

OBEY   TRUTH

PEACE   CROSS

FORGIVE   SIN

HOLY   CHURCH

HEAVEN   LORD

CHURCH DOODLES

Something That Inspired Me From Today's Sermon

SONGS WE SANG TODAY

I'm SO Thankful For:

PRAYER requests

_____
_____
_____
_____
_____
_____

How I Felt About Today's Service

SERMON NOTES

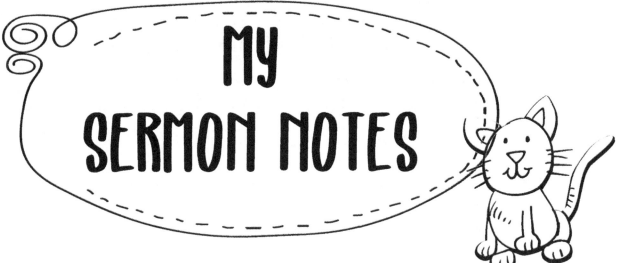

MY SERMON NOTES

Name:_____

date:_____

SPeaKeR:_____

Passages:_____

TODAY'S SERMON IS ABOUT:

_____

_____

_____

_____

SAY WHAT?!
TWO⊛ things i DiDn't understand:

? _____

_____

? _____

_____

WORSHIP WORDS
(COLOR EACH OF THE WORDS YOU HEARD TODAY)

JESUS   LOVE

PRAY   FAITH

BIBLE   GOD

OBEY   TRUTH

PEACE   CROSS

FORGIVE   SIN

HOLY   CHURCH

HEAVEN   LORD

CHURCH DOODLES

Something That Inspired Me From Today's Sermon

🎵 SONGS WE SANG TODAY

I'm SO Thankful For:

PRAYER requests

_____
_____
_____
_____
_____
_____

How I Felt About Today's Service

SERMON NOTES

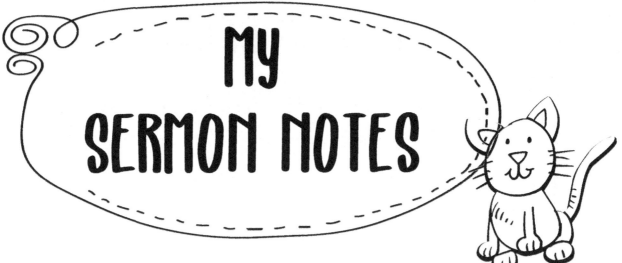

MY SERMON NOTES

Name:_____   Speaker:_____
date:_____   passages:_____

TODAY'S SERMON IS ABOUT:

Say WHAT?!
TWo☻ things i DiDN't UNDerstand:

? _____
_____

? _____
_____

WORSHIP WORDS
(COLOR EACH OF THE WORDS YOU HEARD TODAY)

JESUS   LOVE
PRAY   FAITH
BIBLE   GOD
OBEY   TRUTH
PEACE   CROSS
FORGIVE   SIN
HOLY   CHURCH
HEAVEN   LORD

CHURCH DOODLES

Something That Inspired Me From Today's Sermon

SONGS WE SANG TODAY

I'm SO Thankful For:

PRAYER requests

_____
_____
_____
_____
_____
_____

How I Felt About Today's Service

SERMON NOTES

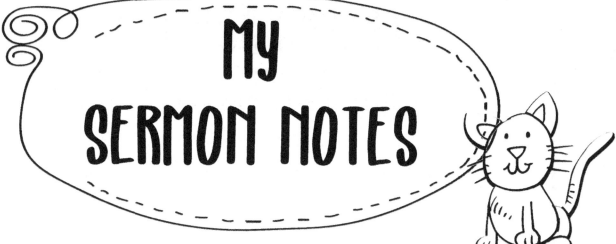

MY SERMON NOTES

Name:_____   Speaker:_____
date:_____   passages:_____

TODAY'S SERMON IS ABOUT:

Say WHAT?!
Two⊛ things i didn't understand:

? _____

? _____

WORSHIP WORDS
(COLOR EACH OF THE WORDS YOU HEARD TODAY)

JESUS   LOVE
PRAY   FAITH
BIBLE   GOD
OBEY   TRUTH
PEACE   CROSS
FORGIVE   SIN
HOLY   CHURCH
HEAVEN   LORD

CHURCH DOODLES

Something That Inspired Me From Today's Sermon

SONGS WE SANG TODAY

I'm SO Thankful For:

PRAYER requests

_____
_____
_____
_____
_____
_____
_____

How I Felt About Today's Service

SERMON NOTES

MY SERMON NOTES

Name:_____ SPEAKER:_____

date:_____ passages:_____

TODAY'S SERMON IS ABOUT:

SAY WHAT?!
Two★ things i Didn't understand:

? _____

_____

? _____

_____

WORSHIP WORDS
(COLOR EACH OF THE WORDS YOU HEARD TODAY)

JESUS   LOVE

PRAY   FAITH

BIBLE   GOD

OBEY   TRUTH

PEACE   CROSS

FORGIVE   SIN

HOLY   CHURCH

HEAVEN   LORD

CHURCH DOODLES

Something That Inspired Me From Today's Sermon

SONGS WE SANG TODAY

I'm SO Thankful For:

PRAYER requests

_____
_____
_____
_____
_____
_____

How I Felt About Today's Service

SERMON NOTES

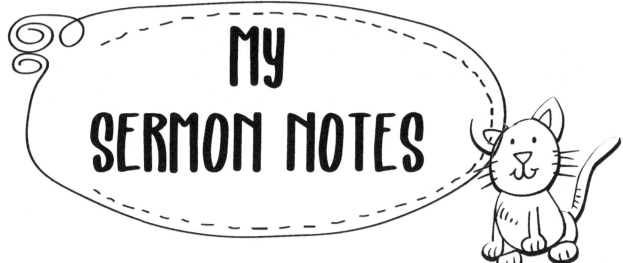

MY SERMON NOTES

Name:_____ SPEAKER:_____

date:_____ passages:_____

TODAY'S SERMON IS ABOUT:

SAY WHAT?!
TW⊛ things i Didn't understand:

?
?

WORSHIP WORDS
(COLOR EACH OF THE WORDS YOU HEARD TODAY)

JESUS   LOVE
PRAY   FAITH
BIBLE   GOD
OBEY   TRUTH
PEACE   CROSS
FORGIVE   SIN
HOLY   CHURCH
HEAVEN   LORD

CHURCH DOODLES

Something That Inspired Me From Today's Sermon

SONGS WE SANG TODAY

I'm SO Thankful For:

PRAYER requests

_____
_____
_____
_____
_____
_____

How I Felt About Today's Service

SERMON NOTES

MY SERMON NOTES

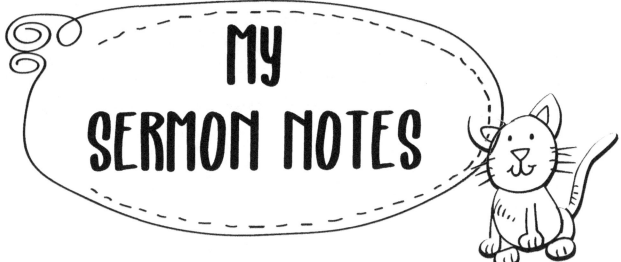

NAME:_____

DATE:_____

SPEAKER:_____

PASSAGES:_____

TODAY'S SERMON IS ABOUT:

Say WHAT?!
TWO★ things i DIDN'T UNDERSTAND:

?

?

WORSHIP WORDS
(COLOR EACH OF THE WORDS YOU HEARD TODAY)

JESUS	LOVE
PRAY	FAITH
BIBLE	GOD
OBEY	TRUTH
PEACE	CROSS
FORGIVE	SIN
HOLY	CHURCH
HEAVEN	LORD

CHURCH DOODLES

Something That Inspired Me From Today's Sermon

SONGS WE SANG TODAY

I'm SO Thankful For:

PRAYER requests

_____
_____
_____
_____
_____
_____

How I Felt About Today's Service

SERMON NOTES

MY SERMON NOTES

Name:_____

date:_____

Speaker:_____

passages:_____

TODAY'S SERMON IS ABOUT:

Say WHAT?!
Two★ things i DiDn't understand:

? _____

? _____

WORSHIP WORDS
(COLOR EACH OF THE WORDS YOU HEARD TODAY)

JESUS   LOVE

PRAY   FAITH

BIBLE   GOD

OBEY   TRUTH

PEACE   CROSS

FORGIVE   SIN

HOLY   CHURCH

HEAVEN   LORD

CHURCH DOODLES

Something That Inspired Me From Today's Sermon

SONGS WE SANG TODAY

I'm SO Thankful For:

PRAYER requests

_____
_____
_____
_____
_____
_____

How I Felt About Today's Service

SERMON NOTES

_____
_____
_____
_____
_____
_____
_____
_____
_____
_____
_____
_____
_____
_____
_____
_____
_____
_____
_____
_____
_____
_____
_____
_____
_____
_____
_____

MY SERMON NOTES

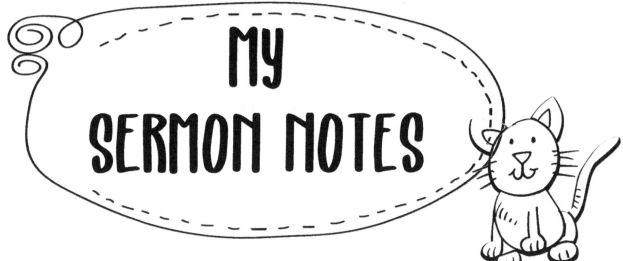

Name:_____   Speaker:_____
date:_____   passages:_____

TODAY'S SERMON IS ABOUT:

_____
_____
_____
_____

Say WHAT?!
Two✷ things i Didn't understand:

?_____

?_____

WORSHIP WORDS
(COLOR EACH OF THE WORDS YOU HEARD TODAY)

JESUS   LOVE
PRAY   FAITH
BIBLE   GOD
OBEY   TRUTH
PEACE   CROSS
FORGIVE   SIN
HOLY   CHURCH
HEAVEN   LORD

CHURCH DOODLES

Something That Inspired Me From Today's Sermon

SONGS WE SANG TODAY

I'm SO Thankful For:

PRaYeR requests

_____
_____
_____
_____
_____
_____

How I Felt About Today's Service

SERMON NOTES

MY SERMON NOTES

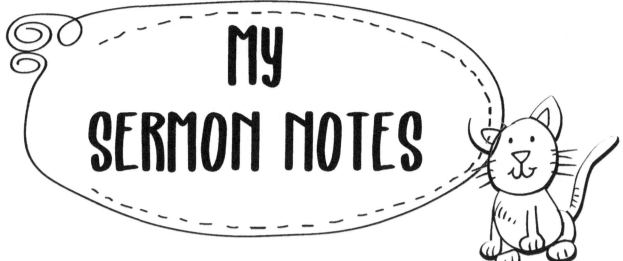

Name:_____

date:_____

speaker:_____

passages:_____

TODAY'S SERMON IS ABOUT:

SAY WHAT?!
TWO⊛ things i didn't understand:

?

?

WORSHIP WORDS
(COLOR EACH OF THE WORDS YOU HEARD TODAY)

JESUS   LOVE

PRAY   FAITH

BIBLE   GOD

OBEY   TRUTH

PEACE   CROSS

FORGIVE   SIN

HOLY   CHURCH

HEAVEN   LORD

CHURCH DOODLES

Something That Inspired Me From Today's Sermon

SONGS WE SANG TODAY

I'm SO Thankful For:

PRAYER requests

_____

_____

_____

_____

_____

_____

How I Felt About Today's Service

SERMON NOTES

MY SERMON NOTES

Name: _____

date: _____

speaker: _____

passages: _____

TODAY'S SERMON IS ABOUT:

SAY WHAT?!
Two things i didn't understand:

? _____
_____
_____

? _____
_____
_____

WORSHIP WORDS
(COLOR EACH OF THE WORDS YOU HEARD TODAY)

JESUS	LOVE
PRAY	FAITH
BIBLE	GOD
OBEY	TRUTH
PEACE	CROSS
FORGIVE	SIN
HOLY	CHURCH
HEAVEN	LORD

CHURCH DOODLES

Something That Inspired Me From Today's Sermon

SONGS WE SANG TODAY

I'm SO Thankful For:

PRAYER requests

_____
_____
_____
_____
_____
_____

How I Felt About Today's Service

SERMON NOTES

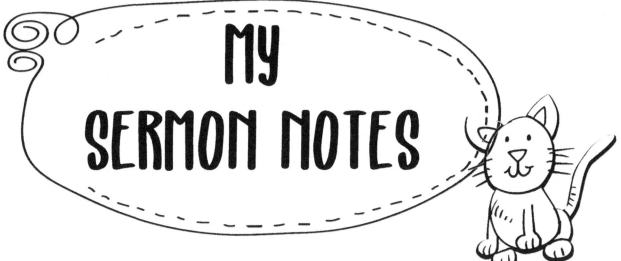

MY SERMON NOTES

Name:_____   Speaker:_____

date:_____   passages:_____

TODAY'S SERMON IS ABOUT:

Say WHAT?!
TW⊛ things i didn't understand:

? _____

? _____

WORSHIP WORDS
(COLOR EACH OF THE WORDS YOU HEARD TODAY)

JESUS   LOVE

PRAY   FAITH

BIBLE   GOD

OBEY   TRUTH

PEACE   CROSS

FORGIVE   SIN

HOLY   CHURCH

HEAVEN   LORD

CHURCH DOODLES

Something That Inspired Me From Today's Sermon

SONGS WE SANG TODAY

I'm SO Thankful For:

PRAYER requests

_____
_____
_____
_____
_____
_____

How I Felt About Today's Service

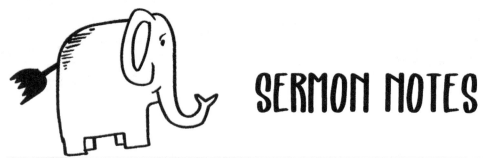

SERMON NOTES

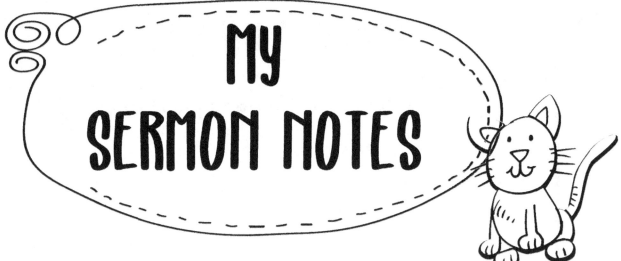

MY SERMON NOTES

Name:_____

date:_____

Speaker:_____

passages:_____

TODAY'S SERMON IS ABOUT:

Say WHAT?!
Two⊛ things i DiDN't UNDERSTAND:

? _____
_____
_____

? _____
_____

WORSHIP WORDS
(COLOR EACH OF THE WORDS YOU HEARD TODAY)

JESUS   LOVE
PRAY   FAITH
BIBLE   GOD
OBEY   TRUTH
PEACE   CROSS
FORGIVE   SIN
HOLY   CHURCH
HEAVEN   LORD

CHURCH DOODLES

Something That Inspired Me From Today's Sermon

SONGS WE SANG TODAY

I'm SO Thankful For:

PRAYER requests

How I Felt About Today's Service

SERMON NOTES

MY SERMON NOTES

Name:_____ Speaker:_____
date:_____ passages:_____

TODAY'S SERMON IS ABOUT:

Say WHAT?!
Two★ things i DIDN'T understand:

?_____
_____
_____
?_____
_____

WORSHIP WORDS
(COLOR EACH OF THE WORDS YOU HEARD TODAY)

JESUS   LOVE
PRAY   FAITH
BIBLE   GOD
OBEY   TRUTH
PEACE   CROSS
FORGIVE   SIN
HOLY   CHURCH
HEAVEN   LORD

CHURCH DOODLES

Something That Inspired Me From Today's Sermon

SONGS WE
SANG TODAY

I'm SO Thankful For:

PRAYER requests

_____
_____
_____
_____
_____
_____

How I Felt About Today's Service

SERMON NOTES

_____

_____

_____

_____

_____

_____

_____

_____

_____

_____

_____

_____

_____

_____

_____

_____

_____

_____

_____

_____

_____

_____

_____

_____

_____

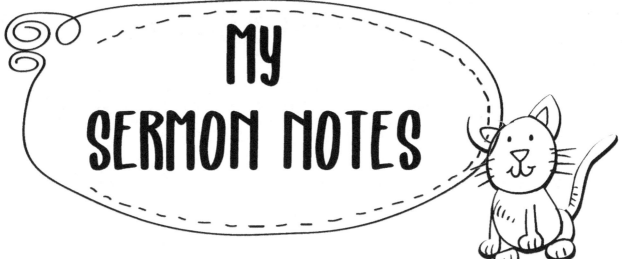

MY SERMON NOTES

NAME:_____

DATE:_____

SPEAKER:_____

PASSAGES:_____

TODAY'S SERMON IS ABOUT:

_____

_____

_____

_____

SAY WHAT?!
TWO⊛ things i DiDN't understand:

? _____

? _____

WORSHIP WORDS
(COLOR EACH OF THE WORDS YOU HEARD TODAY)

JESUS   LOVE
PRAY   FAITH
BIBLE   GOD
OBEY   TRUTH
PEACE   CROSS
FORGIVE   SIN
HOLY   CHURCH
HEAVEN   LORD

CHURCH DOODLES

Something That Inspired Me From Today's Sermon

SONGS WE SANG TODAY

I'm SO Thankful For:

PRAYER REQUESTS

_____
_____
_____
_____
_____

How I Felt About Today's Service

SERMON NOTES

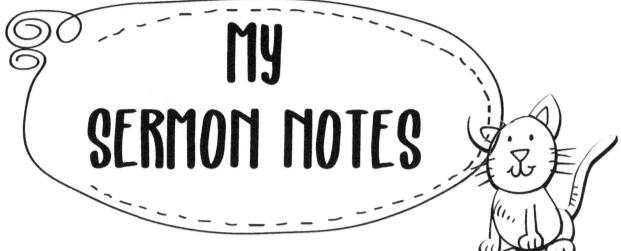

MY SERMON NOTES

Name:_____ Speaker:_____
date:_____ passages:_____

TODAY'S SERMON IS ABOUT:

Say WHAT?!
Two⊛ things i DiDn't understand:

? _____
_____
_____

? _____
_____
_____

WORSHIP WORDS
(COLOR EACH OF THE WORDS YOU HEARD TODAY)

JESUS	LOVE
PRAY	FAITH
BIBLE	GOD
OBEY	TRUTH
PEACE	CROSS
FORGIVE	SIN
HOLY	CHURCH
HEAVEN	LORD

CHURCH DOODLES

Something That Inspired Me From Today's Sermon

SONGS WE SANG TODAY

I'm SO Thankful For:

PRAYER requests

_____

_____

_____

_____

_____

_____

How I Felt About Today's Service

SERMON NOTES

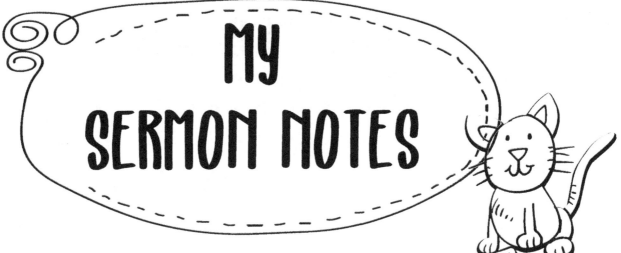

MY SERMON NOTES

Name:_____

date:_____

SPEAKER:_____

passages:_____

TODAY'S SERMON IS ABOUT:

_____

_____

_____

_____

SAY WHAT?!
Tw⊛ things i DiDn't understand:

? _____

_____

? _____

_____

WORSHIP WORDS
(COLOR EACH OF THE WORDS YOU HEARD TODAY)

JESUS   LOVE

PRAY   FAITH

BIBLE   GOD

OBEY   TRUTH

PEACE   CROSS

FORGIVE   SIN

HOLY   CHURCH

HEAVEN   LORD

CHURCH DOODLES

Something That Inspired Me From Today's Sermon

SONGS WE SANG TODAY

I'm SO Thankful For:

PRAYER requests

_____
_____
_____
_____
_____

How I Felt About Today's Service

SERMON NOTES

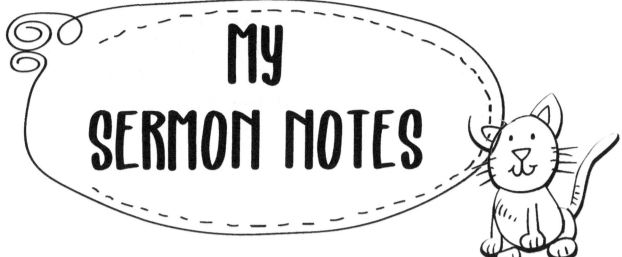

MY SERMON NOTES

Name:_____

date:_____

Speaker:_____

passages:_____

TODAY'S SERMON IS ABOUT:

Say WHAT?!
TWO⊛ things i DiDN't UNDERSTAND:

?

?

WORSHIP WORDS
(COLOR EACH OF THE WORDS YOU HEARD TODAY)

JESUS   LOVE

PRAY   FAITH

BIBLE   GOD

OBEY   TRUTH

PEACE   CROSS

FORGIVE   SIN

HOLY   CHURCH

HEAVEN   LORD

CHURCH DOODLES

Something That Inspired Me From Today's Sermon

SONGS WE SANG TODAY

I'm SO Thankful For:

PRAYER requests

_____
_____
_____
_____
_____
_____

How I Felt About Today's Service

SERMON NOTES

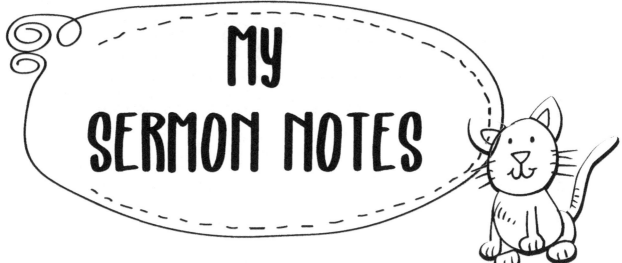

MY SERMON NOTES

Name:_____   Speaker:_____
date:_____   passages:_____

TODAY'S SERMON IS ABOUT:

Say WHAT?!
Two✷ things i DiDn't unDerstanD:

? _____
_____
_____
? _____
_____

WORSHIP WORDS
(COLOR EACH OF THE WORDS YOU HEARD TODAY)

JESUS   LOVE
PRAY   FAITH
BIBLE   GOD
OBEY   TRUTH
PEACE   CROSS
FORGIVE   SIN
HOLY   CHURCH
HEAVEN LORD

CHURCH DOODLES

Something That Inspired Me From Today's Sermon

SONGS WE SANG TODAY

I'm SO Thankful For:

PRAYER requests

_____
_____
_____
_____
_____
_____

How I Felt About Today's Service

SERMON NOTES

MY SERMON NOTES

NAME:_____   SPEAKER:_____
DATE:_____   PASSAGES:_____

TODAY'S SERMON IS ABOUT:

_____

_____

_____

_____

SAY WHAT?!
Two★ things i didn't understand:

? _____

? _____

WORSHIP WORDS
(COLOR EACH OF THE WORDS YOU HEARD TODAY)

JESUS   LOVE

PRAY   FAITH

BIBLE   GOD

OBEY   TRUTH

PEACE   CROSS

FORGIVE   SIN

HOLY   CHURCH

HEAVEN   LORD

CHURCH DOODLES

Something That Inspired Me From Today's Sermon

SONGS WE SANG TODAY

I'm SO Thankful For:

PRAYER requests

_____
_____
_____
_____
_____
_____

How I Felt About Today's Service

SERMON NOTES

MY SERMON NOTES

Name:_____

date:_____

Speaker:_____

Passages:_____

TODAY'S SERMON IS ABOUT:

Say WHAT?!
Two⊛ things i Didn't Understand:

?

?

WORSHIP WORDS
(COLOR EACH OF THE WORDS YOU HEARD TODAY)

JESUS   LOVE

PRAY   FAITH

BIBLE   GOD

OBEY   TRUTH

PEACE   CROSS

FORGIVE   SIN

HOLY   CHURCH

HEAVEN   LORD

CHURCH DOODLES

Something That Inspired Me From Today's Sermon

SONGS WE SANG TODAY

I'm SO Thankful For:

PRAYER requests

_____
_____
_____
_____
_____
_____

How I Felt About Today's Service

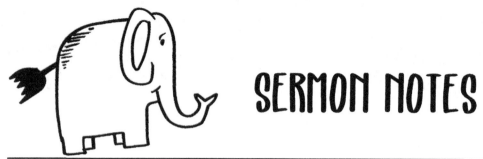

SERMON NOTES

MY SERMON NOTES

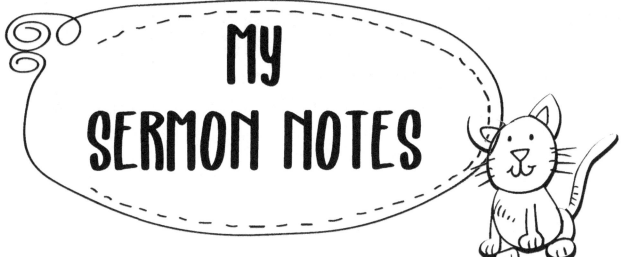

Name:_____   Speaker:_____
date:_____   passages:_____

TODAY'S SERMON IS ABOUT:

Say WHAT?!
TWO⊛ things i DiDn't unDerstanD:

? _____
       _____
       _____
? _____
       _____
       _____

WORSHIP WORDS
(COLOR EACH OF THE WORDS YOU HEARD TODAY)

JESUS   LOVE
PRAY   FAITH
BIBLE   GOD
OBEY   TRUTH
PEACE   CROSS
FORGIVE   SIN
HOLY   CHURCH
HEAVEN   LORD

CHURCH DOODLES

Something That Inspired Me From Today's Sermon

SONGS WE SANG TODAY

I'm SO Thankful For:

PRAYER requests

_____
_____
_____
_____
_____
_____

How I Felt About Today's Service

SERMON NOTES

MY SERMON NOTES

Name:_____

date:_____

SPEAKER:_____

Passages:_____

TODAY'S SERMON IS ABOUT:

_____

_____

_____

_____

SAY WHAT?!
TWO things i DiDN't UNDERSTAND:

? _____

_____

? _____

_____

WORSHIP WORDS
(COLOR EACH OF THE WORDS YOU HEARD TODAY)

JESUS   LOVE

PRAY   FAITH

BIBLE   GOD

OBEY   TRUTH

PEACE   CROSS

FORGIVE   SIN

HOLY   CHURCH

HEAVEN   LORD

CHURCH DOODLES

Something That Inspired Me From Today's Sermon

SONGS WE SANG TODAY

I'm SO Thankful For:

PRAYER requests

_____
_____
_____
_____
_____
_____

How I Felt About Today's Service

SERMON NOTES

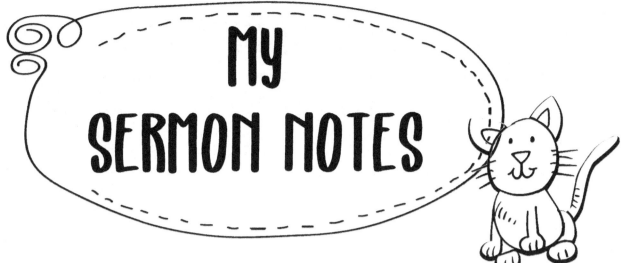

MY SERMON NOTES

Name:_____

date:_____

Speaker:_____

Passages:_____

TODAY'S SERMON IS ABOUT:

_____

_____

_____

_____

SAY WHAT?!
TWO things i DIDN'T understand:

? _____

_____

? _____

_____

WORSHIP WORDS
(COLOR EACH OF THE WORDS YOU HEARD TODAY)

JESUS   LOVE

PRAY   FAITH

BIBLE   GOD

OBEY   TRUTH

PEACE   CROSS

FORGIVE   SIN

HOLY   CHURCH

HEAVEN   LORD

CHURCH DOODLES

Something That Inspired Me From Today's Sermon

SONGS WE SANG TODAY

I'm SO Thankful For:

PRAYER requests

_____
_____
_____
_____
_____
_____

How I Felt About Today's Service

SERMON NOTES

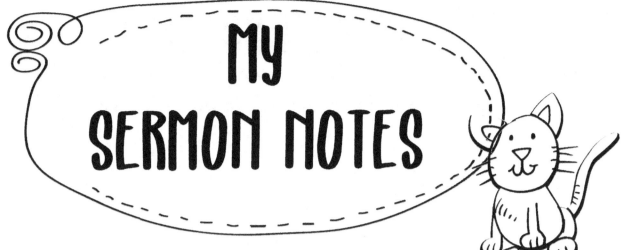

MY SERMON NOTES

Name: _____

date: _____

speaker: _____

passages: _____

TODAY'S SERMON IS ABOUT:

Say WHAT?!
TWO✱ things i DIDN'T understand:

? _____

? _____

WORSHIP WORDS
(COLOR EACH OF THE WORDS YOU HEARD TODAY)

JESUS   LOVE

PRAY   FAITH

BIBLE   GOD

OBEY   TRUTH

PEACE   CROSS

FORGIVE   SIN

HOLY   CHURCH

HEAVEN   LORD

CHURCH DOODLES

Something That Inspired Me From Today's Sermon

SONGS WE SANG TODAY

I'm SO Thankful For:

PRAYER REQUESTS

_____
_____
_____
_____
_____
_____

How I Felt About Today's Service

SERMON NOTES

_____

_____

_____

_____

_____

_____

_____

_____

_____

_____

_____

_____

_____

_____

_____

_____

_____

_____

_____

_____

_____

_____

_____

MY SERMON NOTES

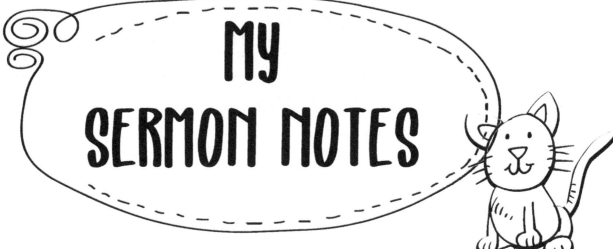

Name:_____

date:_____

Speaker:_____

Passages:_____

TODAY'S SERMON IS ABOUT:

SAY WHAT?!
Tw✷ things i didn't understand:

?

?

WORSHIP WORDS
(COLOR EACH OF THE WORDS YOU HEARD TODAY)

JESUS	LOVE
PRAY	FAITH
BIBLE	GOD
OBEY	TRUTH
PEACE	CROSS
FORGIVE	SIN
HOLY	CHURCH
HEAVEN	LORD

CHURCH DOODLES

Something That Inspired Me From Today's Sermon

SONGS WE SANG TODAY

I'm SO Thankful For:

pRAYER requests

_____
_____
_____
_____
_____
_____

How I Felt About Today's Service

SERMON NOTES

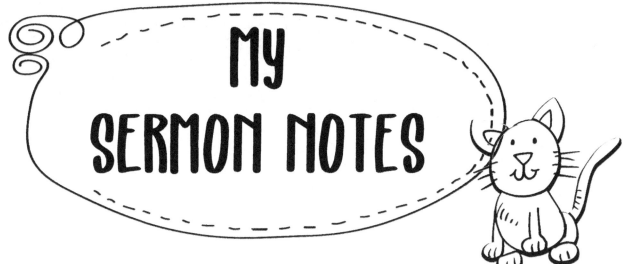

MY SERMON NOTES

Name:_____

date:_____

speaker:_____

passages:_____

TODAY'S SERMON IS ABOUT:

_____

_____

_____

_____

Say WHAT?!
TWO things i DIDn't understand:

? _____

_____

? _____

_____

WORSHIP WORDS
(COLOR EACH OF THE WORDS YOU HEARD TODAY)

JESUS	LOVE
PRAY	FAITH
BIBLE	GOD
OBEY	TRUTH
PEACE	CROSS
FORGIVE	SIN
HOLY	CHURCH
HEAVEN	LORD

CHURCH DOODLES

Something That Inspired Me From Today's Sermon

SONGS WE SANG TODAY

I'm SO Thankful For:

PRaYer requests

_____
_____
_____
_____
_____
_____

How I Felt About Today's Service

SERMON NOTES

_____

_____

_____

_____

_____

_____

_____

_____

_____

_____

_____

_____

_____

_____

_____

_____

_____

_____

_____

_____

_____

_____

_____

_____

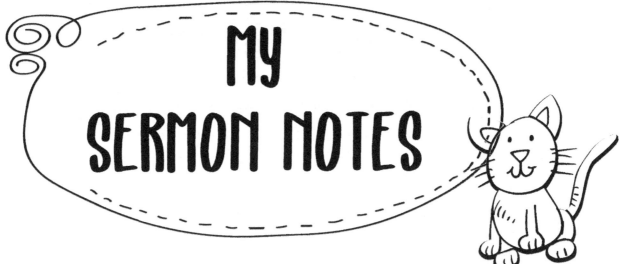

MY SERMON NOTES

Name:_____   Speaker:_____
date:_____   passages:_____

TODAY'S SERMON IS ABOUT:
- -
- -
- -
- -

Say WHAT?!
Two✷ things i DiDn't unDerstanD:

? _____
_____
_____
? _____
_____

WORSHIP WORDS
(COLOR EACH OF THE WORDS YOU HEARD TODAY)

JESUS   LOVE
PRAY   FAITH
BIBLE   GOD
OBEY   TRUTH
PEACE   CROSS
FORGIVE   SIN
HOLY   CHURCH
HEAVEN LORD

CHURCH DOODLES

Something That Inspired Me From Today's Sermon

SONGS WE SANG TODAY

I'm SO Thankful For:

PRAYER requests

_____
_____
_____
_____
_____

How I Felt About Today's Service

SERMON NOTES

MY SERMON NOTES

Name: _____

date: _____

speaker: _____

passages: _____

TODAY'S SERMON IS ABOUT:

_____

_____

_____

_____

Say WHAT?!
Tw⊛ things i DiDn't understand:

? _____

? _____

WORSHIP WORDS
(COLOR EACH OF THE WORDS YOU HEARD TODAY)

JESUS   LOVE

PRAY   FAITH

BIBLE   GOD

OBEY   TRUTH

PEACE   CROSS

FORGIVE   SIN

HOLY   CHURCH

HEAVEN   LORD

CHURCH DOODLES

Something That Inspired Me From Today's Sermon

SONGS WE
SANG TODAY

I'm SO Thankful For:

PRAYER requests

_____
_____
_____
_____
_____
_____

How I Felt About Today's Service

SERMON NOTES

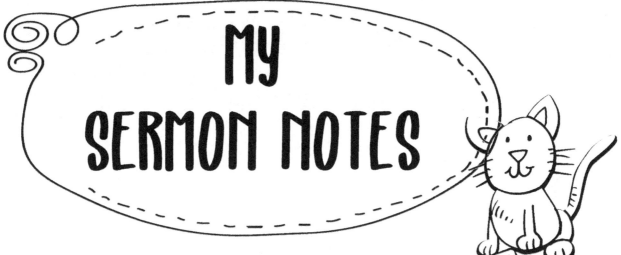

MY SERMON NOTES

Name:_____   Speaker:_____

date:_____   passages:_____

TODAY'S SERMON IS ABOUT:

SaY WHAT?!
Two⊛ things i didn't understand:

? _____
  _____

? _____
  _____

WORSHIP WORDS
(COLOR EACH OF THE WORDS YOU HEARD TODAY)

JESUS   LOVE

PRAY   FAITH

BIBLE   GOD

OBEY   TRUTH

PEACE   CROSS

FORGIVE   SIN

HOLY   CHURCH

HEAVEN   LORD

CHURCH DOODLES

Something That Inspired Me From Today's Sermon

SONGS WE SANG TODAY

I'm SO Thankful For:

PRAYER requests

_____
_____
_____
_____
_____
_____

How I Felt About Today's Service

SERMON NOTES

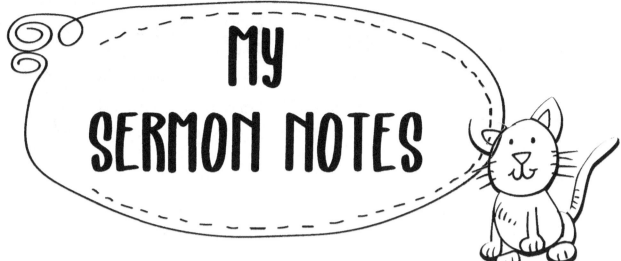

MY SERMON NOTES

Name:_____   Speaker:_____
date:_____   passages:_____

TODAY'S SERMON IS ABOUT:

Say WHAT?!
TWO⊛ things i DiDn't UnDerstand:

? _____
 _____
? _____
 _____

WORSHIP WORDS
(COLOR EACH OF THE WORDS YOU HEARD TODAY)

JESUS   LOVE
PRAY   FAITH
BIBLE   GOD
OBEY   TRUTH
PEACE   CROSS
FORGIVE   SIN
HOLY   CHURCH
HEAVEN   LORD

CHURCH DOODLES

Something That Inspired Me From Today's Sermon

SONGS WE SANG TODAY

I'm SO Thankful For:

PRAYER requests

_____
_____
_____
_____
_____
_____

How I Felt About Today's Service

SERMON NOTES

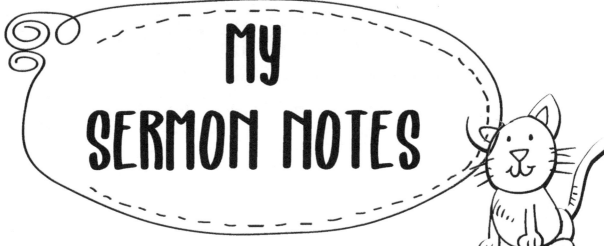

MY SERMON NOTES

NAME:_____

DATE:_____

SPEAKER:_____

PASSAGES:_____

TODAY'S SERMON IS ABOUT:

SAY WHAT?!
TWO⊛ things i DIDN'T UNDERSTAND:

?

?

WORSHIP WORDS
(COLOR EACH OF THE WORDS YOU HEARD TODAY)

JESUS   LOVE
PRAY   FAITH
BIBLE   GOD
OBEY   TRUTH
PEACE   CROSS
FORGIVE   SIN
HOLY   CHURCH
HEAVEN   LORD

CHURCH DOODLES

Something That Inspired Me From Today's Sermon

SONGS WE SANG TODAY

I'm SO Thankful For:

PRAYER requests

_____

_____

_____

_____

_____

_____

How I Felt About Today's Service

SERMON NOTES

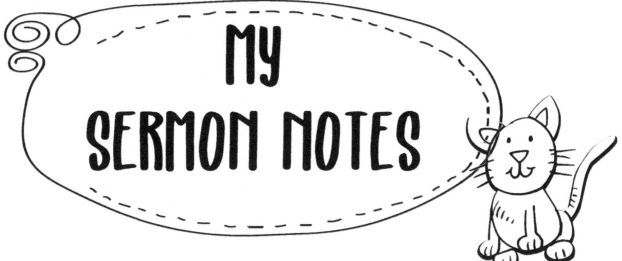

MY SERMON NOTES

Name:_____   Speaker:_____

date:_____   passages:_____

TODAY'S SERMON IS ABOUT:

Say WHAT?!
TWO things i DiDn't UnDerStand:

? _____

? _____

WORSHIP WORDS
(COLOR EACH OF THE WORDS YOU HEARD TODAY)

JESUS   LOVE
PRAY   FAITH
BIBLE   GOD
OBEY   TRUTH
PEACE   CROSS
FORGIVE   SIN
HOLY   CHURCH
HEAVEN   LORD

CHURCH DOODLES

Something That Inspired Me From Today's Sermon

SONGS WE
SANG TODAY

I'm SO Thankful For:

pRAYeR requests

_____
_____
_____
_____
_____
_____

How I Felt About Today's Service

SERMON NOTES

MY SERMON NOTES

Name:_____ Speaker:_____

date:_____ passages:_____

TODAY'S SERMON IS ABOUT:
_____
_____
_____
_____

SAY WHAT?!
Two⊛ things i DiDn't understand:

? _____
_____

? _____
_____

WORSHIP WORDS
(COLOR EACH OF THE WORDS YOU HEARD TODAY)

JESUS   LOVE
PRAY   FAITH
BIBLE   GOD
OBEY   TRUTH
PEACE   CROSS
FORGIVE   SIN
HOLY   CHURCH
HEAVEN   LORD

CHURCH DOODLES

Something That Inspired Me From Today's Sermon

SONGS WE SANG TODAY

I'm SO Thankful For:

PRAYER requests

_____
_____
_____
_____
_____
_____

How I Felt About Today's Service

SERMON NOTES

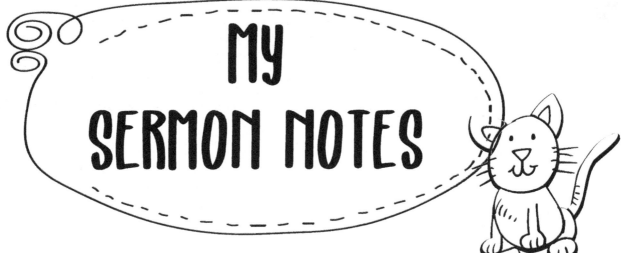

MY SERMON NOTES

Name:_____

date:_____

SPeakeR:_____

passages:_____

TODAY'S SERMON IS ABOUT:

_____

_____

_____

_____

Say WHAT?!
TWO✸ things i DiDN't UNDERStand:

?

?

WORSHIP WORDS
(COLOR EACH OF THE WORDS YOU HEARD TODAY)

JESUS   LOVE

PRAY   FAITH

BIBLE   GOD

OBEY   TRUTH

PEACE   CROSS

FORGIVE   SIN

HOLY   CHURCH

HEAVEN   LORD

CHURCH DOODLES

Something That Inspired Me From Today's Sermon

SONGS WE SANG TODAY

I'm SO Thankful For:

PRAYER requests

_____
_____
_____
_____
_____
_____

How I Felt About Today's Service

SERMON NOTES

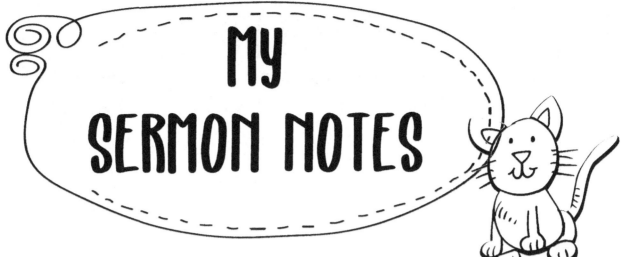

MY SERMON NOTES

Name:_____

date:_____

Speaker:_____

passages:_____

TODAY'S SERMON IS ABOUT:

Say WHAT?!
Two⊛ things i DiDn't understand:

? _____

_____

? _____

_____

WORSHIP WORDS
(COLOR EACH OF THE WORDS YOU HEARD TODAY)

JESUS   LOVE
PRAY   FAITH
BIBLE   GOD
OBEY   TRUTH
PEACE   CROSS
FORGIVE SIN
HOLY CHURCH
HEAVEN LORD

CHURCH DOODLES

Something That Inspired Me From Today's Sermon

SONGS WE
SANG TODAY

I'm SO Thankful For:

PRAYER requests

_____
_____
_____
_____
_____
_____

How I Felt About Today's Service

SERMON NOTES

_____
_____
_____
_____
_____
_____
_____
_____
_____
_____
_____
_____
_____
_____
_____
_____
_____
_____
_____
_____
_____
_____
_____
_____
_____
_____
_____

Made in the USA
Middletown, DE
04 September 2022

73208448R00117